Diamonds Spell Danger

Annie Broadhead
and Ginni Light

Diamonds Spell Danger

ELT

For Jai

PENGUIN BOOKS

Published by the Penguin Group
27 Wrights Lane, London W8 5TZ, England
Viking Penguin Inc., 40 West 23rd Street, New York, New York 10010, USA
Penguin Books Australia Ltd, Ringwood, Victoria, Australia
Penguin Books Canada Ltd, 2801 John Street, Markham, Ontario, Canada L3R 1B4
Penguin Books (NZ) Ltd, 182–190 Wairau Road, Auckland 10, New Zealand

Penguin Books Ltd, Registered Offices: Harmondsworth, Middlesex, England

First published by Penguin Books 1989
13579108642

Copyright © Annie Broadhead and Ginni Light, 1989
All rights reserved
Illustrations by Richardson Freelance

Typeset in 11/14pt Linotron 202 Zapf Book Light

Made and printed in Great Britain by
Hazell Watson & Viney Limited
Member of BPCC plc
Aylesbury, Bucks, England

CONTENTS

INTRODUCTION

Adventure Gamebooks allow readers to take part in their own story. At the end of many of the sections readers are asked to make a choice. They then turn to the relevant section to continue their own particular story.

Each book consists of a series of interwoven short stories. Readers will not usually read the whole of each book, but, by making their own choices, read one of the short stories.

Readers can then go back and make different choices and give their story a different direction. In this way the book can be extended, or reused, and the stories become quite different.

DIAMONDS SPELL DANGER

Your grandfather disappeared in very strange circumstances, while he was on a trip to England. No one knows what happened to him. No one ever answers any questions about him. Several members of the family have tried to find your grandfather because he took with him the priceless Konchi Diamond and everyone wants it back.

During a dream you heard a voice. It told you that you must go to England and discover what happened to him. You know he was last seen in a village called Harminster, on the coast. You decide to go to England to solve the mystery. Success or failure depends on you and the decisions you make.

1

You arrive in the charming fifteenth-century village of Harminster late on a Friday night. The only place to stay is the local hotel which is a large rambling Tudor house.

On Saturday morning you tell the hotel manager that you are trying to solve the mystery of your grandfather's disappearance but you do not tell him about the Diamond. He looks horrified and tells you that sometimes it is better not to ask too many questions. When you insist, the only thing he tells you is that there was some connection with the Castle. The Castle is very old and now stands empty. It was once owned by a local nobleman. The manager tells you it is impossible to get to the house now as the coastal road has almost fallen into the sea. If you decide to ignore his advice and look for the Castle, turn to **27**. If you decide to talk to some other people first to get more information, turn to **36**.

2

You wake up with a most awful headache. You are lying on a damp floor, your wrists are tied and you have a smelly handkerchief in your mouth. You try to remember what happened and why you are in this dangerous situation. You are rather puzzled and confused at first, then your memory comes back. Oh dear! How are you to get out of this? Someone is obviously very interested in your search for your grandfather and the Konchi Diamond. You feel in your pocket, by rolling from side to side, that the stone is still there. In fact, it seems to be giving out a very intense light which allows you to see your surroundings.

It is a very strange light which seems to have unusual powers because when you hear a rustling sound and move so that you can see what it is, the light beam from the stone focuses itself on the direction of the sound. The light beam picks out a mouse and seems to immobilize it. In fact, it seems to hypnotize it. If only you could get your hands free, you could try and use the stone's power to help you. What can you do? Turn to **81**.

3

You decide to climb over the wall. The wall is quite high so climbing over it is not as easy as it looks. The wall is covered with plants, ivy and moss. Eventually you find a couple of footholds in the crumbling wall. You pull yourself up and manage to sit on top of the wall.

When you look at the garden, you cannot believe

your eyes. There is a beautiful rose garden. What is surprising is the fact that it is well looked after. The grass has been cut, the roses have been pruned and somebody has been doing the weeding, but who? The Castle is supposed to be uninhabited now.

You slide down the other side of the wall and begin to walk around the garden. You want to see if you can find any clues. Who could it be who looks after this garden with such care? Turn to **5**.

4

The figure walks towards you. Suddenly you realize that it is your grandfather. You run towards him, he gives you a big hug and says, 'I'm really happy to see you at last, my boy! But we must hurry because the robbers who murdered my brother are still free and now they're looking for me!'

You are really pleased to see him but, of course, you know that there is something seriously wrong. You start to say, 'But why are you here hiding in this cellar? Where are we anyway?' You have so many questions that you would like answered. The gypsy interrupts you and says to your grandfather, 'Let me explain as I'm involved, too.'

He nods and she continues, 'It all started when your grandfather came to visit his brother, Jorge, and brought the Konchi Diamond with him. Many people

tried to steal it because it is not only valuable but has magical powers, too. None of them succeeded because the Diamond is cursed! Only your family can keep it, anyone who steals it dies, or some disaster happens to them. The Konchi Diamond only brings good luck to your family but death to everyone else, sooner or later!'

Your grandfather interrupts her, 'Well, this time robbers almost succeeded in getting it. They murdered my brother and would have murdered me to get it but my friend, the gypsy, managed to hide it and I escaped through the secret tunnel. I've been hiding here in the Castle ever since.'

You ask, 'Where is the Konchi Diamond?'

Your grandfather replies, 'It is in the Manor House in the ...'

Suddenly, you hear loud footsteps running down the stairs and towards the cellar. Turn to **80**.

5

As you walk around the garden, you find evidence of very recent work. In one corner someone has been digging and the garden fork has been left out. You go through an arch of roses and you see a basket with some gardening gloves in it. In another part of the garden you can see a circular white summer-house. You go towards it and find that the door is open. Inside there are two comfortable old armchairs and a wooden table.

You begin to wonder if the Castle is, in fact, uninhabited. It certainly does not look like it. You suddenly feel a little embarrassed. After all, perhaps you are trespassing on someone else's property. What if they come and find you here? How can you explain what you are doing? If you go back over the wall the same way you came, turn to **24**. If you go on towards the Castle, turn to **13**.

6

You are lying on the ground. Your head really hurts, you realize that someone must have hit you on the head. But who and why? You remember the stone and immediately put your hand into your pocket. It has vanished! Whoever it was knew who you were. They also knew what they wanted. You try to sit up, your head is swimming, you think you are going to black out. You lie down again on the hard ground. You hear Miss Lyon calling you, you just manage to say, 'I'm here! Help! Help!' Then, everything goes black again.

When you wake up again, you are in hospital and a policeman is sitting beside the bed. When he sees that you are conscious, he starts talking to you and asking you lots of questions.

You try to answer them, but even to you, your story sounds very strange. You came to England to look for your grandfather, you accepted a stone from a gypsy that you did not know, you had tea with a lady you had never met before, then at her home you got hit on the head by someone that you did not see and the stone was stolen!

The policeman obviously thinks you are mad. You wonder if you really are! Turn to **43**.

7

The policeman says you must go with him to the police station. He is obviously very angry with you. He thinks you are young, stupid and irresponsible. In the police station, you begin to tell your story. The policeman is getting angrier and angrier. After a few minutes he shouts, 'I've never heard such a ridiculous story in all my life. Looking for a lost grandfather, indeed! Don't you know those cliffs are dangerous? There is a big sign saying, "KEEP OUT". You've lost your passport and ticket as well, have you? Well, I'll just have to phone your Embassy.'

He leaves you alone in this little room. You are very upset. He is away for a long time.

When he eventually comes back, he says, 'Well, that's settled then. A police car will take you to pick up your luggage from the hotel. Then it'll take you

to London, to the Embassy. They will give you a temporary identity card and a ticket for the next flight home. Goodbye. Perhaps this will teach you not to make up fantastic stories in the future.' This is the end of the adventure for you. You have no choice. You go back home with the mystery still unsolved. ■

8

As you go along the path on the left, it gets narrower and narrower. The path winds into the small wood which is in front of the Castle.

Even though it is a warm summer's day it feels cool and damp in the wood. It is also quite dark. A shiver runs down your back and you feel as if you are being watched. You tell yourself it is only your imagination. Then you hear the 'crack' of a branch being broken. There must be someone else in the wood and they have trodden on a branch. No, it could be an animal. You stand still for a moment to see if you can hear anything. The only thing you can hear is the pounding of your own heart. Your breathing seems very loud.

At last you come to the other side of the wood and there is the Castle in front of you. Its tall grey walls are covered with ivy. There are lots of towers and turrets. The shutters are closed over all the windows. There is a large diamond-shaped lawn in front of the Castle. You cross it. Turn to **45**.

You and Miss Lyon are so frightened that you stand there paralysed with fear. You cannot move. The footsteps come nearer and nearer. Your hearts are thumping. The door opens and two policemen come in. They say, 'What are you doing here? We received a very strange phone call. Someone told us to go and investigate funny goings-on at this derelict castle – and we find you!'

You both try to give reasonable explanations to the policemen to explain why you are there but even to you, they sound ridiculous.

The policemen say to you, 'Now, hop in the car and we'll give you a lift back to the village. Come on, Miss Lyon, it's time you were tucked up safely in bed and as for you, young man! You really should know better than to . . .' They talk on and on in the car. You and Miss Lyon are both sound asleep within minutes!

In the next few days, you find it impossible to do anything. The police seem to be following you everywhere. Miss Lyon finds the same thing is happening to her. Obviously, something is going on but you cannot find out what it is, you decide that enough is enough and that someone else in your family can take the responsibility for finding your grandfather and the Konchi Diamond! You still have the stone, after all! You decide to fly back home! This is the end of the road for you! ■

10

You decided that you could not ask the gardener any of the questions you are dying to ask. You are certainly not going to solve any mystery, or find your grandfather, or the Konchi Diamond, if you continue like this! You are certainly not going to be a good detective unless you try a bit harder to be brave and adventurous. Why not try and be a little bit more like James Bond? Well, this is the end of the road for you. You could turn back to **84** and try a different route.

11

As you enter the shop, a bell above the door rings. The girl looks up from her work and says, 'I'll be with you in a minute, I'd just like to finish this stone.'

'That's all right,' you say, 'I'm just looking.' You look at the creamy blue opals and the pure blue of the lapis lazuli. On the work-bench next to the girl there are some diagrams of cut diamonds.

Suddenly you see one which looks exactly like the Konchi Diamond and there is a red cross next to it. You begin, 'I don't suppose you ever get the chance to cut diamonds do you?'

The girl laughs and says, 'I'm still training for the job. I'd be scared to death working on a priceless

diamond. This shop belongs to my father actually. I'm learning from him. It's funny you should mention diamonds though. About a month ago a man came into the shop and asked us if we could make a replica of a diamond – you know, make a fake. Then he got this incredible diamond out of his pocket to show us.'

'Who was he?' you ask.

'It was Lord Fairchild. He used to live in the Castle here in Harminster,' the girl replies.

'And did you make a replica of the diamond?' you ask.

'Yes, we did. He came and picked it up a few days later. That's all I know about it though,' she replies. You ask her if she has Lord Fairchild's address and she says she has. If you go to Lord Fairchild's address, turn to **67**. If you go to the Castle, turn to **45**.

12

Your grandfather answers, 'Well, I don't have it! When I realized that robbers were after the Diamond, I had a replica made and the robbers took that!'

'But where's the original?' you ask.

'I don't know! I gave it for safe keeping to a good friend, a rather strange friend actually.'

'But how could you do that? Where is it now?' you ask.

Miss Lyon has started laughing and laughing. You and your grandfather both stare at her and wonder if the experience she has just been through has been too much for her.

When she can finally manage to speak, she says, 'You've got it! You've had it all the time! The gypsy gave it to you! She knew who you were immediately! Normal stones don't have the power of the Konchi Diamond!'

Of course, she is right! You pull the stone out of your pocket, it is vibrating and sending out a warm beam of light that fills the whole room. Well, this is the end of the adventure for you, you have found your grandfather and the Konchi Diamond has found you! Well done! But you could not have done it without the gypsy and Miss Lyon!

13

You find an old gate in the wall. This must lead from the secret garden to the Castle. There is a large handle which easily turns. You open the gate cautiously. Just as you go through the gate, a hand grabs your shoulder and a voice shouts, 'Caught you!'

You look round and see an old man. He has a very wrinkled face, half his teeth are missing, his back is bent and he is dressed in very shabby clothes.

When you turn round and the old man sees your

face, his eyes nearly pop out of his head. 'Well, well, you must be Arthur's son. The family resemblance is unmistakable. Have you brought a message for me?' the old man asks as he grabs you even more tightly.

'I don't know what you are talking about. Who's Arthur? What message?' you reply. Even though the old man is still holding you tightly he is not very strong. You could easily pull yourself free and run away. If you run away, turn to **41**. If you stay and talk to him and try and get some more information, turn to **16**.

14

You decide not to tell the Embassy official any more. On the one hand you feel a bit stupid telling people about the Konchi Diamond and your grandfather, and on the other hand, if the Embassy cannot find him, what chance have you? The official leaves the room for a moment. When he comes back he says, 'We think the best thing for you is to go back home as soon as possible. This is a serious business and we don't want you to become involved. We are dealing with dangerous people. We have arranged for you to take the 10 a.m. flight back home tomorrow morning. Thank you. Goodbye.' This is the end of the adventure for you. ■

15

You decide to go back to the hotel. The easiest way is to walk along the beach until you get to the village. Anyway you do not fancy climbing up the cliff again.

When you get back to the hotel you think you should inform the police about your bag and your lost papers.

When you get to reception, the receptionist hands you a message which has been left for you. This is very strange because no one knows you are here. The message reads: *'You lost your bag today – let this be an omen. Go back home or else the next time you could lose your life!'*

If you decide to give up and go back home, turn to **29**. If this message makes you even more determined to solve the mystery, turn to **58**.

16

'Who is Arthur?' you ask the old man.

'Arthur, we call him Arthur, that's his English name,' the old man explains, 'came to the village to visit Lord Fairchild. It seems there's some connection between the two families. They both have a huge diamond in the middle of their coat of arms. Years ago, Lord Fairchild lived in the Castle. While Arthur

was staying with Lord Fairchild at the Castle, some burglars came and stole all the family treasures. This broke Lord Fairchild's heart. In fact he moved away from the Castle.

'Of course the burglars soon found out that Arthur was a close friend of Lord Fairchild's. They even managed to find out about Arthur's priceless Diamond. They started threatening Arthur and Lord Fairchild. They said that if Arthur gave them the Konchi Diamond, they would give Lord Fairchild all his possessions back.

'I haven't seen Arthur or Lord Fairchild for a long time now but before Arthur disappeared he asked me to look after the Castle grounds and in particular this walled garden. I always think Arthur will send me a message or something to let me know what's happening. That's why I thought he'd sent you.

'Anyway why don't you walk round the Castle and see if you can discover anything?' You decide to do this. Turn to **45**.

17

The gypsy frightens you. You cannot explain why. How can she know what you are looking for? Surely, it is just a coincidence that she is offering you a stone which resembles the Konchi Diamond? Anyway, you turn away from the stall and walk towards the other side of the square. As you walk, you can feel the eyes of the gypsy following you. You begin to think again. It is true that you look a lot like your grandfather. Perhaps the gypsy recognized you as a member of the family. Perhaps she can help solve the mystery. If you change your mind and go back to the gypsy for the stone, turn to **55**. If you decide your first decision to walk away was right, turn to **60**. If you decide to try and find out something about the gypsy, turn to **78**.

18

You start walking away from the Castle with the policeman. As you walk, the policeman says nothing. This seems very strange to you. You begin to look sideways at him. He looks very odd. Yes, in fact, his uniform does not fit him at all. It is much too small. You then notice that he is wearing brown shoes which do not go with his uniform. His shirt and tie do not look right either.

Suddenly you realize he is not a policeman at all. By now you are coming to the edge of the wood. If you run away from this man now, turn to **64**. If you continue walking with him, turn to **76**.

19

You decided to change the subject and talk about something else. The stone that had become hot in your hand again becomes like ice. You decided you did not really feel ready to trust Miss Lyon, the old lady.

Well, if you cannot trust an old lady, who can you trust? You certainly have not found many other clues and she seems to provide the only lead, so far.

It would be a good idea to reconsider your decision and ask her a few very direct questions. As soon as you have decided to ask Miss Lyon for information, the stone becomes warm again in your hand. You are on the right path. Turn to **77**.

20

The receptionist seems quite friendly so you decide to ask her about Professor Higgins, Richard and Miss Lyon. She tells you that Professor Higgins is a retired university professor. He spends all his time reading Shakespeare. Richard is a young man who, in fact, has just left Harminster to go and work in London. Miss Lyon is an elderly lady who spends all her time looking after her roses. You decide that none of these can be the person who wrote the message. There is nothing you can do. ■

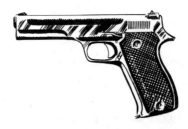

21

You push through the bushes. This is very difficult and the bushes scratch your arms and legs badly. Your leg begins to bleed. After a while the bushes get smaller and it is easier to get through. You continue in the direction of the road. Eventually you see a field and then a high stone wall. When you reach the field, you feel quite happy.

However, you realize that you are already quite tired and hungry. You sit down in the field to rest. Your leg hurts. It is still bleeding so you tie your

handkerchief around it like a bandage. This feels much better and you are rather proud of yourself.

While you are sitting here, you look at the wall again and realize this must be the wall which surrounds the Castle. You feel excited now you are so close to the Castle and decide to continue. When you reach the wall, it is rather high and you cannot see a door or a gate. If you decide to climb over the wall, turn to **3**. If you decide to walk round the wall until you find a gate, turn to **44**.

22

The best thing is to sort out all your papers; apply for a new passport; report the loss of your airline ticket; get some money transferred from home to a London bank. You decide to go to the Embassy first as you know it could take a long time to sort out your passport.

When you arrive at the Embassy, you have to fill out a form. You complete it, hand it in and then you have to wait. After about five minutes a very official-looking man comes out from the office, walks straight towards you and says, 'Would you mind coming into my office for a moment please?'

You think this is a bit odd because many other people have been waiting much longer than you. Once inside the office, the man says, 'Do take a seat.

I was particularly interested in your form because a certain member of your family has been reported missing. I presume it must be your grandfather. Do you know anything about this?'

'No one in our family has heard anything about him for quite a long time, but I didn't know that he had been officially reported missing,' you reply. Again you are not sure how much to say to this Embassy official.

'It could be even more serious. We believe your grandfather may have been carrying a valuable diamond. Is this true?' he asks. If you tell him all about the Konchi Diamond, turn to **61**. If you decide not to tell him about the Konchi Diamond, turn to **14**.

23

Everyone else runs through the door and into the tunnel. You alone cannot move. You are too frightened. The main door into the cellar opens and two evil-looking men with guns in their hands run in. They laugh horribly when they see you standing there, frozen with fear. 'We weren't exactly looking for you but now that the others have escaped, we'll take you instead!' one of them says. They come over to you and grab you by the arms. You struggle and try to escape. The other robber says, 'Hold still or

we'll shoot you! We've already done away with one of your family so another one doesn't make any difference.'

You gasp with horror as you realize that these two cruel men must be your great-uncle's murderers. How on earth are you going to manage to escape from them? Turn to **52**.

24

You suddenly get cold feet. Your sense of adventure, courage and daring deserts you. You must be mad, climbing over walls to trespass on someone else's property. The wall is much more difficult to climb up from this side. You finally manage to get up but you have broken all your finger-nails and grazed your hands and knees. Once on top of the wall again, you see that you are not exactly at the same place as before. Here you will have to jump down into thick bushes and all sorts of undergrowth. Just then you hear a dog barking. It has seen you and comes running towards you barking and snarling. What are you going to do? You cannot just sit there and wait until it goes away. That could be hours.

Then you hear someone coming through the bushes. A man appears in a policeman's uniform. You are not sure whether to be relieved or afraid.

'What do you think you are doing here?' the

policeman asks. 'The Castle is strictly private; nobody is allowed to go in there. I'm going to take you back to the police station with me,' he says. Turn to **18**.

25

You are walking towards the wood. You see a glimpse of something red amongst the trees. Somebody is definitely there. Could it be the gypsy?

You call out, 'Hello! Hello! Who's there?' You feel a bit silly but also extremely jumpy.

To your surprise, out of the woods walks the old lady you met at the market. She is quite small, quite old and rather dumpy. She is dressed in a very English way, with a string of pearls around her neck and clothes that are very typical of an elderly Englishwoman.

She says to you, 'Oh! It's you! I rather thought it would be! Ever since Arthur disappeared, I've been coming here regularly for my evening walks. You look so much like him, I almost thought it was him. Let's go for a stroll together and talk.'

You feel very relieved that it was an old, if rather eccentric, lady that you met in the woods, and not a ghost, so you agree and you go for a walk around Devil's Point, talking all the way. You have lots of questions to ask, of course. For instance, who is this Arthur that you resemble so closely? Turn to **54**.

26

You go back to the village. By the time you arrive at the hotel, you are really tired and hungry. You go to your room and have a shower. If you eat here at the hotel, you will be able to ask the manager or the waitress more about the Castle. This seems a good plan.

When you have finished your dinner it is quite quiet in the hotel. The waitress brings you some coffee. You say to her, 'By the way, I walked towards the Castle today, could you tell me about it? I mean, who lived there and where have they gone? Do you know anything about the coat of arms there? I'm fascinated by that sort of thing, you know.'

Instantly the waitress looks down, as though hiding some terrible secret. She mutters, 'I don't know anything about it.' Then she goes away. Turn to **48**.

27

It is still quite early as you set out to find the Castle. The sun is shining and there is a nice breeze coming in from the sea. For a while you manage to forget your grandfather's disappearance and enjoy the English countryside. At first you manage to follow the coastal road without difficulty, but after a short time the road becomes difficult to follow and very narrow.

Suddenly you find yourself dangerously near the edge of the cliff. Carefully approaching the edge of the cliff, you see the road has fallen into the sea and you can see parts of the road smashed on the rocks below. Straight ahead, the road is covered with thick bushes and undergrowth. If you decide to try to get through this, turn to **21**. If you are going to climb down the cliffs and walk along the beach, turn to **53**.

28

You again hear someone trying to attract your attention. 'Psst, psst! Over here!'

You roll from side to side to the other end of the damp cellar towards the sound. To your surprise, you find Miss Lyon hiding behind a large box. The room is full of boxes that look as though they have been there for centuries.

'Do try and come a bit closer, then I can untie your hands,' she says. 'I thought you were Arthur's son or more likely his grandson, but now I'm sure. I've seen that strange light before. Lie still, then I can untie your hands.' You obediently do as she says. She unties your hands, removes the smelly handkerchief from your mouth and then you both move quietly towards the door. You take the stone out of your

pocket and its strange light guides you. The stone feels as though it has a life of its own. It is pulling you.

You feel rather frightened but at the same time incredibly excited. Miss Lyon has suddenly become very daring and she says, 'Oh! It's just like old times! I only wish Arthur were here! We used to enjoy ourselves so much having adventures like this!'

Suddenly you hear footsteps approaching. You put the stone back in your pocket. What are you going to do? If you decide to go and hide behind the boxes, turn to **59**. If you find it impossible to move because you are too frightened and you do not know what to do, turn to **9**.

29

You spend the next day reporting the loss of your bag. This is quite difficult to explain.

You want to get out of this place as soon as possible. Ever since you received the message, you feel as though someone is watching you; an enemy or a murderer.

Your Embassy gives you a temporary identity card and you book a flight back home. You remember your grandfather saying, 'Diamonds spell Danger' when talking about the Konchi Diamond.

People will do anything for money. It is much safer for you to go home. This is the end of your adventure. ■

30

The gypsy is holding open the small door leading to the tunnel or secret passage. You all just have the time to get into the tunnel and bolt the door firmly behind you. The gardener switches on his torch and you hurry down the damp narrow tunnel, back the way you came, to the Manor House. You all run as fast as you can. By the time you have reached the opening in the fireplace at the other end of the tunnel, you are all out of breath.

Once you are in the room, the gardener closes the opening in the wood panelling and says, 'We never know when we might need that escape route again.'

You ask your grandfather, 'Where is the Konchi Diamond?'

The gypsy replies, 'Here it is. It's inside this little statue of an ancient Egyptian goddess.' She walks across the room and picks up the statue. She turns it upside down and takes off the base.

Just then, you hear feet running through the house. The door bursts open. Two evil-looking men run into the room. You notice with horror that they are both armed.

'Put your hands up and hand over the statue!' they order.

The gypsy has meanwhile managed to get the Konchi Diamond out of the statue and throws it into the air. Everybody runs to try and catch it. Turn to **47**.

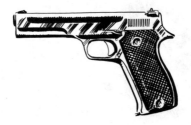

31

You decide to walk to the Castle. It is in fact quite a long way but it is quite a nice day so you keep on walking.

Eventually, as you go across a field, you see a wall. This must be the wall which surrounds the Castle grounds. You cannot see a gate anywhere but you will probably soon find one if you just walk around the wall. Turn to **44**.

32

By this time you are tired and depressed. Perhaps it was not such a good idea to be so impulsive and foolhardy. Anyway you begin to climb back up the cliff. This is much more difficult than you imagined. It takes your last ounce of strength. When you are about half way up, you get stuck. You cannot go on up and you cannot go back down. Fear paralyses you. You do not know what on earth you can do.

Just then you hear a dog barking. Perhaps someone is taking his dog for a walk along the cliffs. You begin to shout, 'Help. Help!'

After a few minutes a voice shouts, 'Hang on, don't be afraid. I'll get help.'

You stay there for what seems ages. Then a rope is thrown over the cliff. Another voice shouts, 'Tie this round your waist and we'll pull you up.' You do as he says. You are pulled up. When you get to the top, you find two policemen and an old man with a dog.

'What are you doing climbing on these cliffs? You must be mad. Don't you know they are dangerous? Who are you? You aren't from the village, are you?' the policeman asks. If you tell the policeman everything about your reasons for being here, turn to **7**. If you just say you were out for a walk and apologize for causing so much trouble, turn to **40**.

33

Here you are at Devil's Point. It took you a long time to get here, and it was difficult. You asked lots of people how to get here and they always gave you the same answer. 'Ooh! I wouldn't go there if I were you! It's a bad place! It's haunted by the ghosts of pirates long since dead and gone!'

It does feel rather sinister – here you are in one of the most desolate places in the whole world. It is completely exposed to the elements, it is very windy and the only vegetation is a small group of trees on the edge of the cliff. The rest is rock and small bushes.

You do not feel like walking up to the trees, they look so dark and the whole place seems to be unfriendly. But you decide that as there seems to be nothing and nobody else here that you might as well walk towards the trees.

As you are walking there, you hear a sudden noise. It sounds very much like a gun going off. You are very nervous and jumpy and you realize that the noise was probably someone in the wood who stepped on a branch or twig. You decide to go and find out who is there even though you feel very frightened. Turn to **25**.

34

You really do not know how to get into the Castle grounds. The gate looks too high to climb. While you are thinking, you look more closely at the coat of arms. You climb up on to the gate so that you can see the coat of arms better. What is the diamond shape in the middle made of? As you touch it there is a click and the lock in the gate springs open. The gate swings open with you still clinging to it.

You jump down into the Castle grounds. At last your adventure will really begin. A secret lock on the gate, how fascinating!

In front of you there are two paths. You cannot see the Castle itself because it is hidden behind some trees. The path on the left looks like a footpath. It is very narrow and dark. The one on the right is wide enough to take a car. If you take the path on the right, turn to **46**. If you take the path on the left, turn to **8**.

35

You are at the gypsy's stall. She has been watching you approach. You feel rather nervous. You hope that she will still give you the stone; you have a strange feeling that this stone will somehow help you in your

search for your grandfather and the Konchi Diamond. You look hopefully at the gypsy, but you cannot really ask her for the stone. Fortunately, she speaks to you and says, 'Ah! So you decided to come back! That was wise. I've been keeping this for you.' Turn to **65**.

36

You leave the hotel and decide to go for a walk in the village to find some other people you can ask for more information about your grandfather. It is a beautiful day, the sun is shining and people are arriving for the Saturday market.

You decide to visit the market and walk around looking at the stalls. Suddenly, you notice a stall selling antique jewellery. You stop, because you have seen a box which contains a lot of uncut precious stones. You remember the Konchi Diamond and look more closely at the stall. A woman is sitting behind the table. She looks like a gypsy; she is wearing very brightly-coloured clothes and lots of jewellery. She sees you and gasps. She says, 'I know what you are looking for. It isn't here but take this stone to help you!'

Another stallholder who has been watching, calls to you: 'Don't take it. I wouldn't trust her if I were you!'

She holds out the stone for you to take. If you decide to accept the stone, turn to **65**. If you decide not to accept the stone, turn to **17**.

37

You close the door and go along the corridor a little way until you come to a very large kitchen. There are various little rooms off it, a couple of store-rooms, a laundry room and so on. You are not really sure which direction to go in. You happen to look down at the floor. It is a tiled floor and in the design of the tiles you once again see the shape of a diamond. As you look at this, it seems to be pointing to one of the doors. You go over to it. When you open the door there is a flight of stairs obviously going down into the cellars.

There are several rooms down here. You think you can hear the sound of some slight movements. Is someone down here or are there rats? You are really scared, it is dark and damp and smelly. You can hear

your own heart thumping. There it is again. The sound is much clearer this time.

You go into one of the cellars. There, on the floor, is your grandfather. His hands and legs are tied and his mouth is gagged. You cannot believe it. You rush over to him and untie him. Turn to **85**.

38

Well, you decided that you did not particularly want to speak to the gardener. You feel rather foolish; you are trespassing on someone else's land and you do not really know whether you are doing anything to try and trace your grandfather and the Konchi Diamond. You feel as though your trip to England was rather wasted. What have you managed to discover so far? How are you going to discover anything when you are so timid? You know there must be some people who can help you. Turn back to **36** and try again! Have the courage of your own convictions.

39

You decided to find out what you can from the old lady, so you start chatting to her. She introduces herself as Miss Lyon. Soon she is telling you all about the history of the village, stories about the local butcher, baker, farmer and so on, back to the year dot for all you know. Suddenly, she says something which makes you prick up your ears:

'And then this very elegant and distinguished man arrived and things began to change. Because, you see, until then, nothing exciting had ever happened here! But from that point on, Arthur – '

You say, 'Oh! Please, carry on. What did he look like? What did he do? Where did he come from?' She looks amused at your obvious interest and says, 'Steady on, please, young man! I was just rambling, of course. But, if you are really interested, perhaps you'd care to come and have tea with me tomorrow. At around six, shall we say?'

You are in quite a difficult situation. On the one hand, you would very much like to go and have tea with this rather odd lady but on the other hand, you would also like to go to Devil's Point, it sounds mysterious and very interesting. If you decide to go and have tea with Miss Lyon, turn to **86**. If you decide to refuse the invitation to tea and go straight to Devil's Point on the following day, turn to **33**.

40

One of the policemen asks if you are all right. You say, 'Yes thank you. I'm all right really. I'm ever so sorry for causing so much trouble. I think I'd better go back to my hotel now.'

'Ah, so you're staying in the village, are you?' asks the policeman. 'That's good. We'll walk back with you,' he says.

Finally you reach the hotel and the policemen leave you alone. When you are in your room, you begin to think over what has happened. The worst thing is losing your passport. You can easily replace your ticket and other papers. To replace your passport you will have to go to London to your Embassy. It could take days to sort this out. If you go to London the next day to sort out your passport, turn to **22**. If you stay in the village and try to solve the mystery of your grandfather, turn to **73**.

41

You pull yourself free. It is very easy to get away from the old man. You start to run. The old man shouts, 'Wait, don't go. I'm a friend. I can help you, come back!'

You do not believe him. Where are you going to run? You cannot go on to the Castle and investigate because the old man will follow you. It was a stupid thing to do, to run away. Go back to **21** and try again.

42

You decided that you did not trust the gardener enough to go with him. You really are very timid, you should try to be a bit braver.

This is no ordinary holiday you are having, you *are* trying to find both your grandfather and the Konchi Diamond. You have had two clues to follow, two people who obviously know something of interest to you. Go back to **1** and try again.

43

The policeman's questions have exhausted you. You thankfully go back to sleep, trying to ignore a very bad headache. Obviously, that part of your story is real enough.

When you wake up again some hours later, the same policeman is sitting beside your bed. You think,

'Oh, no! I don't think I can stand answering all those questions again! The more I try to explain the situation, the crazier it sounds!'

He says, 'Come on, young man. Get dressed. I'm going to give you a lift.'

You answer him, 'That's very kind of you. But where to?'

He replies, 'To the airport, of course. I telephoned your Embassy who contacted your family. Your family insists that you take the next plane back home! So that's why I'm taking you to the airport.'

What a disaster! You feel you really cannot explain yourself very well at the moment and you decide you might as well go home. This adventure was a bit of a non-starter. You found out quite a lot but not enough and with a headache that feels as if your head is going to explode, you are in no condition to continue your search. You decide to go home and return another time when you feel better! ■

44

You start to walk around the wall; there must be a gate somewhere. After about fifteen minutes, you come to an enormous iron gate. It is very high, heavy and beautifully decorated. In the middle of the wrought-iron gate there is a coat of arms. When you look more closely at this, you see, in the middle, the

shape of a huge diamond. It is exactly the shape of
the Konchi Diamond. Ah! Your imagination is
running away with you. This shape must be common
in such ancient designs.

You want to go into the garden. You look down at
the lock on the gate. It does not look too old and
rusty but when you push the gate it is definitely
locked. You push and push and nothing happens. If
you decide to go back to the village because you are
tired and you want to ask about the owner of the
Castle, turn to **26**. If you continue to try to get into
the Castle grounds, turn to **34**.

45

You begin to walk around the Castle. You are looking
for a window or a door where you can get in. The
presence of your grandfather seems to be very strong.
Something seems to be urging you to go on, to look,
to find him.

You go round the Castle. At the back, you find a
small door. It is an old oak door and in the middle
there is a diamond shape. You suddenly realize the
diamond is showing you the way. You touch the
diamond shape, it turns and the door opens. You go
in. If you close the door so that no one will notice
anything unusual, turn to **37**. If you leave the door
open, turn to **71**.

46

The path on the right takes you around the wood which is in front of the Castle. This seems to be a very long way round. On your left is the wood and on your right a field. You keep wondering whether you should have taken the other path. Perhaps if you go into the wood now, you will be able to find the other path.

Just then, very close by in the wood you hear a gunshot. It makes you jump. You are surprised that someone else is in the Castle grounds. But why not? It could be a poacher shooting birds or rabbits. You are glad you did not go into the wood, it might have been dangerous.

Then there is another shot. You are sure the shot was fired from the wood – and in your direction! Then there is another shot, and then another. The shots are definitely aimed at you. They are not meant to hit you and kill you but they are certainly warning shots.

You turn and run back the way you came. You decide this is too dangerous. You cannot get involved with people who are prepared to shoot you. You decide to go back home. This is the end of your adventure. ■

47

You are all trying to catch the Konchi Diamond. The Diamond is doing very strange things. It is hovering in the air and giving out a very strong white light. It seems to be vibrating. You walk towards it.

Suddenly, you hear the sound of heavy footsteps running towards the room. The two robbers point their guns at the door just as several armed police-men enter.

The gypsy, who has been watching, begins to speak loudly and gutturally in a strange language. Everyone watches her, transfixed. She points with both hands at the two robbers and you somehow know that she is cursing them with an ancient and terrible curse. They drop their guns on the floor and slowly, like robots, they raise their hands above their heads and walk towards the policemen. The policemen have been watching these strange events in total disbelief. They handcuff the robbers immediately.

One of them says, 'I can't believe this, even though

I've seen it with my own eyes. If someone had told me this had happened to them, I'd have thought they'd gone mad!' Turn to **75**.

48

Out of the corner of your eye you see the waitress go into the manager's office. You have a feeling she is going to tell him about your questions. You are right. After about five minutes the manager comes out of his office. You can tell he is angry by the way he slams the door and by the look on his face. He comes straight up to you and says, 'I hear you've been asking questions about the Castle and annoying my staff.'

He is almost shouting. You are glad there are not

other people in the dining room now as this is really embarrassing. 'I'm sorry, I really don't know what you mean,' you manage to stammer.

'I'm talking about your idiotic questions about the Castle. Don't come here stirring up trouble. In fact I'd rather you left the hotel. Make sure you leave by 10 a.m. tomorrow. And if I see you in the village again . . .' he shouts as he walks off.

There is nowhere else to stay in the village and anyway the manager has really upset you. You do not know why you have made him so angry but you decide it is better to leave. This is the end of your adventure. ■

49

You decided to ignore the strange noise but unfortunately, Miss Lyon does not. She gets up and walks to the front door and opens it.

She calls out, 'Who is it? Who's there?' She asks you, 'Can you see anyone?' You get up and reluctantly go and look too. She asks you to walk round the cottage and have a look. You do as she asks, feeling rather let down that your interesting conversation has been interrupted at such a crucial point. You walk around the back of the house and suddenly you are aware that there really is someone there, watching you.

You feel really frightened and turn round to walk back to the front of the house. As you do this, you feel a sharp bang on your head, you see stars, then nothing. Turn to **6**.

50

A few minutes later, you both hear the sound of running feet. It sounds like a whole army! Over a megaphone, a voice calls, 'You are surrounded! Come out, with your hands up!' It is the police. Miss Lyon had called the police.

The two criminals stare at you both with hatred. The one called Jim says, 'We'll get you, just wait! When we come out of prison, we'll come looking for you and your grandfather!'

'You won't be out of prison for a long time!' says Miss Lyon and then calls, 'In here!' to the policemen.

In a matter of seconds, the room is full of police. They arrest the robbers and push them out of the room. Fortunately, you just had time to slip the stone back into your pocket before the police came in!

The police take you and Miss Lyon to her cottage, tell you that they will call back in the morning to take statements and leave you, advising you to go to bed. Miss Lyon turns to you and says, 'Come on in. You're staying with me tonight. There's someone waiting anxiously to see you.'

'Who is it?' you ask. You have so many questions you want to ask that you do not know where to begin.

Miss Lyon smiles mysteriously at you and says, 'Come and see for yourself!' Turn to **69**.

51

You walk up to the gardener. He stands up and waits for you to approach. As you get nearer, you notice that he looks a bit like the gypsy at the market; in fact, as you get nearer and nearer, the more he looks like the gypsy. He has the same dark, troubled eyes and he looks at you without surprise, almost as if he has been expecting you. You say, 'Hello! I just happened to notice the house and I thought it was so beautiful that I'd come and have a closer look and . . .'

You are just talking for the sake of talking because you feel quite embarrassed and quite nervous, the gardener says. 'I've been waiting for you. I knew you would come sooner or later! Have you met my sister yet? She's been waiting for you, too.'

You start to say, 'Who's your sister?', then you realize it is a stupid question. You know that his sister must be the gypsy at the market.

He smiles at you and says, 'You *have* met my sister. She asked me to show you something in case you didn't trust her enough.'

He walks ahead of you, round to the back of the house, and goes in at the back door. You have no alternative, you must follow him. You are sure that he is going to show you something which will help to solve the mystery. Turn to **84**.

52

The two men push you through the main door of the cellar. You really do not know what to do. At the moment, you have no choice, you must go where the two robbers are taking you.

One of them says, 'Come on, hurry up! We must get to the Manor House. We know that the Konchi Diamond is there. We'll use this kid as a hostage.'

You gasp as you realize that they must have heard the last part of the conversation in the cellar, when your grandfather was telling you what had happened.

They pull you through the woods and soon you see the village ahead of you. What can you do? What are those evil men going to do to you? Suddenly, you feel a sharp knock on your head and everything goes black. Turn to **62**.

53

You carefully look over the edge of the cliff. At first it looks quite dangerous, but then you notice a place where you can climb down. As you begin to climb down, some seagulls begin to circle above you. They fly closer and closer and make you feel really scared. Are they going to attack you? One comes so close it makes you lose your balance. In your panic you drop your bag. The bag contains all your papers, including your passport and ticket.

When you left the hotel you did not realize what an adventure this was going to be. You get your balance back but you see it is impossible to get your bag back. It has fallen a long way down between two rocks. You are very disappointed, frustrated and scared.

Eventually, you get down to the beach and begin to walk to one end of the bay. When you get there you see your way is completely blocked by large, dangerous rocks. You cannot continue. If you decide to go back to the top of the cliff, turn to **32**. If you are really unhappy about your bag and the fact that you have lost your passport and ticket, you decide to go back to the hotel. Turn to **15**.

54

You walk along with the rather odd old lady, chatting away animatedly. Finally, you just have to ask her, 'Who is Arthur? Why do you think I'm connected with him?'

She looks at you with a mischievous smile and says, 'I thought you'd never ask! Arthur is a gentleman, well, an old gentleman for you, as old as I am, who arrived here many years ago. I know he came to visit some relative of his but I gather there was also some trouble at home. Anyway, he changed all our lives and brought excitement to this rather sleepy village.'

You say, 'Why, what did he do? What happened?' She replies, 'Arthur seemed to have plenty of money, a lovely personality and lots of interests, but when he came to the village and eventually settled here, there were a lot of strange people who suddenly turned up. Bad people, you know!'

The stone weighs heavily in your pocket and all at once becomes hot in your hand and starts to vibrate as though it is trying to tell you something. In a flash, you realize. Arthur – Arturo – your grandfather's name! It must be one and the same person. So your grandfather *was* here. If you decide to ask the old lady a few more questions, turn to **77**. If you decide to change the subject and talk about something else, turn to **19**.

55

You decided that you had to go back to the gypsy.
Too many questions have been left unanswered. Why
does the stone resemble the Konchi Diamond? How
does she know what you are looking for? Why was
she so surprised to see you? You walk back to the
gypsy's stall. You want to ask her all these questions.
Turn to **35**.

56

You decided that you had to trust the gardener,
otherwise you are going to get no answers at all. You
say, 'All right. I'll come with you!' 'Follow me,' he says
and walks directly towards the fireplace. There are
many flowers carved in the beautiful oak wood
panelling surrounding the fireplace. He presses one
of the flowers and immediately a part of the
panelling swings open to reveal an opening, with
what looks like a small staircase leading downwards.

You gasp in surprise and exclaim, 'I've only read
about things like this in my grandfather's books. I
didn't realize they really existed!'

The gardener says, 'Oh, this has been here a long
time. In earlier days, in times of war, the family
sometimes needed to make a quick escape from their

enemies or they would have been killed. This was their secret passage and only members of the family know about it.' While he is talking, he has moved into the opening and is beckoning you to follow. You follow him and start to go down the steps. The gardener takes a torch out of his pocket, switches it on and then presses a hidden button and the panelling closes behind you.

It is very dark and damp in here, you go down the stairs and find yourself in a narrow tunnel. You can see no daylight at all and you wonder where this strange man is taking you. Turn to **66**.

57

Your conversation with Miss Lyon has been interrupted by strange noises outside the cottage. You get up and walk to the front door and peer out. It is very dark by this time and you can see absolutely nothing. It feels very sinister out there and you are just about to close the door when you hear someone whispering, 'Psst, psst, over here!'

Now you are really frightened, who on earth is that calling you? You know no one here. Suddenly, you hear Miss Lyon say, 'Well, is there anyone out there? What are you doing?'

You turn round and take a step back into the house, ready to close the door behind you, when someone grabs you from behind, dragging you back outside. A rough hand is clamped over your mouth, you are unable to shout or say anything and you are pushed down the garden path. You hear Miss Lyon calling you; you bite the hand that is over your mouth. You just manage to shout, 'Help!' then someone hits you over the head. Turn to **2**.

58

Somebody obviously knows why you are here. The person who sent the message must know about the Konchi Diamond. Perhaps he has the Diamond! You look again at the message. It is written with a fountain pen in green ink. That is quite unusual. You might be able to trace the message writer. You go down to reception and ask, 'Did you see the person who left this message for me?'

'No,' says the receptionist. 'I had to go to the dining-room and when I came back, it was on my desk.' Somebody must have been watching the receptionist and when the moment was right, left the message.

'Was anyone waiting in the lobby?' you ask.

'Yes, there was old Professor Higgins, Richard the antique dealer and Miss Lyon from Rose Cottage. That's all,' answers the receptionist. If you go and try to talk to any of these people, turn to **20**. If you go to the Castle again, turn to **31**.

59

You and Miss Lyon decided to hide behind some of the boxes. The footsteps come nearer and nearer and you hear the door being opened. whoever it is has a torch with them, because a beam of light sweeps the room. You peep out from behind the boxes and you see two men. They look very large, very dirty and very frightening. One of them says, 'I'm sure I saw that nosy old woman creeping around. We'd better have a look and make sure that the kid's still here too.'

The other one says, 'Oh, the kid's here right enough. We gave him a big enough bang on the head to make him sleep for a week. That I'm sure of! Come on then, let's look for the interfering old woman. We don't want anything going wrong now that we've got them all.'

They start walking round the room, shining the light from the torch behind the boxes and into the corners. Your heart is beating so loudly, you are certain they can hear it. You hope that Miss Lyon has managed to hide herself well, she is rather old and not very nimble on her feet. Suddenly, there is the most enormous sneeze. Oh, no! That must be Miss

Lyon. The game is definitely up for both of you now. Turn to **87**.

60

You decided that the gypsy frightens you. You do not want to ask any questions of such a strange person. You walk away and decide to explore the village and its surroundings. Far away, in the distance, you can see a beautiful old manor house which looks as though it has been there for ever. It also looks very familiar, but you cannot think why. Then you remember, at home you have a picture hanging in the sitting-room, which was painted by your grand-father and it is of the same house. You decide to go there and have a closer look at it. Soon you are walking up the long winding driveway. When you get closer to the house, you notice an old gardener working in the flower-beds.

They look typically English, full of old-fashioned roses. You wonder what on earth you are going to say to the old gardener. You do not know how you are going to explain who you are and who or what you are looking for, since you do not even know the name of the house, let alone the name of the family who owns it.

The gardener looks up. He has noticed you. If you decide to walk back down the driveway and pretend you have lost your way, turn to **38**. If you decide to go and talk to the gardener and ask him a few questions, turn to **51**.

61

You begin your story, 'Yes, in fact, I know my grandfather came to England with the Konchi Diamond –'

'Yes, of course,' the Embassy official interrupts, 'everyone in our country has heard of the famous Konchi Diamond. There are many stories about its mysterious properties. Don't they say that as long as it stays in the family it will bring good fortune but once it leaves the family, it will bring nothing but death and disaster?'

'That's right. That's the legend associated with the Konchi Diamond,' you reply. 'Do you know anything about my grandfather? I really want to find him,' you continue.

'We know that he was staying in Harminster at Lord Fairchild's Castle some years ago. After some time your grandfather disappeared and then Lord Fairchild disappeared. At that point we handed over the investigation to Chief Inspector Barnes at Scotland Yard. I think you should go and talk to him,' the Embassy official suggests. You decide to follow this advice. Turn to **82**.

62

You wake up in hospital with a nurse and a policeman sitting beside your bed. You have a terrible headache and you cannot remember anything. You do not know where you are, why you are here, what you are doing or anything. You cannot answer any of the policeman's questions.

Fortunately for you, your passport was in your trouser pocket and soon someone from your Embassy is at the hospital. You ask him why he is there and he explains, 'The police telephoned us and asked us to contact your family. We did this and your family insists that you return home immediately!'

You really have no choice, you have to go home. As you have lost your memory, there is not much point in your continuing this adventure. This is the end of the road for you. Perhaps, you would like to go back to **80** and try a different route.

63

You walk back to where the gypsy was. Oh horrors! The stall is there but the gypsy is not. The stall itself is completely empty and there is no sign that anyone has ever been there. What can you do? Nobody can or will give you any information, so you are rather stuck. You wish you had chosen a different path, then maybe you could have got some information or even held the stone that looked so much like the Konchi Diamond in your hand. Well, you did not. You were not brave enough. This is the end of the road for you. You have not succeeded and soon you are sitting on the plane on your way back home. ■

64

You try to walk as far away from the 'policeman' as possible. When you turn a corner in the path, you decide this is a good moment to run away. There are lots of trees and bushes and you think it would be easier for you than for him to run through these, because you are smaller and more agile.

Suddenly, you run away through the bushes. They rip your clothes and scratch your arms and legs but you don't notice any of these things. The 'policeman' shouts after you, 'Hey, you, what do you think you are doing? Come back here at once!' You keep running. Then you hear him shout, 'I'll find you again, don't worry and the next time you won't get away so easily!'

Eventually you arrive back at the hotel. You are in a terrible state. Your clothes are ruined and you are scared to death. You decide this 'adventure' is far too frightening for you and that you want to go back home again as soon as possible. This is the end of your adventure. ■

65

The gypsy puts a large stone in your hand. Immediately, your hand feels cold, as if you were holding a block of ice. When you look at the stone, you see that the size and shape resemble the Konchi Diamond. A shiver runs through your body. You feel scared and excited. You look up, there are so many questions

you want to ask the gypsy. 'How does she know about the Konchi Diamond? How does she know who I am?' you wonder.

When you see her dark, troubled eyes and the expression on her face, you know you cannot ask her these questions. Perhaps you are just imagining things and there is, in fact, no connection with your grandfather.

Then the gypsy speaks again, 'Tomorrow, at sunset, come to Devil's Point.'

You walk away from the stall with the stone in your hand and decide to go to Devil's Point tomorrow. Turn to **72**.

66

You are still walking along the strange dark tunnel. The walls are not very wide and the roof is so low that you have to lower your head. You seem to have been walking for a very long time. You ask the gardener, 'How much further are we going?'

He whispers to you, 'Ssh! We're nearly there. You must be as quiet as a mouse, you never know who is listening!'

At last you see some light at the end of the tunnel. It widens and you find yourself in front of a half-open door. The door is being held open by the gypsy, the one who offered you the stone at the market.

She says, 'Welcome! We have been waiting for you.' She holds open the door for you and her brother, the gardener, to enter. You walk into a very large cellar which someone has obviously been staying in because there is a bed in the corner and a few old chairs scattered around, as well as some lit candles. There is also a wood-burning stove, as it is very damp and normally it would be impossible for anyone to stay in here for very long. You notice a figure leaning against the wall at the far end of the cellar. You wonder who it is. Turn to **4**.

67

Lord Fairchild now lives in a village about ten miles from Harminster. You decide to go there as soon as possible. The bus bumps along the country lanes and it is difficult to imagine that anything could go wrong on such a beautiful day.

When you arrive at Lord Fairchild's home, you knock at the front door and while you wait, you glance around the beautifully kept rose garden. There is no answer. You look at the perfectly cut lawn and as your eyes turn back to the house, you notice an elderly man peering at you from behind the curtains. You wave at him and he pulls the curtain back more so that he can see you better.

Then you hear footsteps and eventually the front door opens.

'Come in quickly and close the door,' the old man says. His behaviour seems very strange to you but the sense of urgency in his voice makes you do what he says.

'Are you Lord Fairchild?' you begin.

'Yes, yes, of course,' the old man says, 'and you must be Arthur's grandson. I've seen photos of you. Don't worry, everything will be resolved within a matter of hours.'

'Wait a minute, I don't know what you're talking about,' you protest. Turn to **70**.

68

You check into a hotel in London. After just one night the Chief Inspector phones you. He says, 'We're going down to Harminster. Lord Fairchild has arranged to exchange the replica of the Konchi Diamond for your grandfather. He is going to meet

the burglars down at his old Castle there. You can come with us as long as you don't get in the way.'

You are very excited and glad to be involved in such a drama. You pack your things and wait for the police to come and pick you up.

The police arrive at Harminster and organize their trap for the Bray Brothers, the infamous burglars. The police go to the Castle very early and hide in the wood. When the Bray Brothers arrive with your grandfather and Lord Fairchild arrives with the replica of the Konchi Diamond, the police will jump out and arrest the Bray Brothers.

You beg to be allowed to go with the police. They eventually give in and off you go to the Castle. Once you are hidden in the wood, you wait. It seems like a long time. Finally you hear the sound of a car. Out get the Bray Brothers and your grandfather. You can hardly stop yourself from shouting and running to him. Next Lord Fairchild arrives. He gets out of his car and walks towards the Bray Brothers. At this moment the police rush out, grab the Bray Brothers and after a bit of a fight everything is under control.

You run towards your grandfather and hug him. You cannot believe you have found each other. Everyone is safe and the Konchi Diamond is safe too.

'Tell me all about it,' you say to your grandfather.

'Let's go and have a cup of tea and I'll tell you everything. For the moment let's just say, "All's well that ends well." It's good to see you my boy,' your grandfather says.

69

You walk into Miss Lyon's cottage and there, sitting in the armchair by the fire, is your grandfather.

After you have greeted each other he tells you what happened.

Apparently when he came to England with the Konchi Diamond, he really came to visit his cousin, Lord Fairchild, the owner of the Castle. Because your grandfather liked England so much and because there had been family troubles at home, he decided to stay, not in the Castle itself because it had not been lived in for a long time, but in the area. Your grandfather continues, 'The Castle is actually where those two robbers took you and where my dear friend, Miss Lyon, found both you and me. I was kidnapped by those robbers and –'

'But why were you kidnapped?' you ask him.

'Because of the Konchi Diamond! People have always wanted to possess it and, as you know, it has magical powers. It brings good luck to our family but disaster to others. Everyone who has tried to steal it has died.'

You ask him, 'But how did you get away from the robbers?'

Miss Lyon answers for him, 'The police rescued him just before they rescued us! The robbers were planning to kill both of you because they realized that when you started asking questions in the village,

they would be caught sooner or later. And when Arthur disappeared and then you did too, I thought the obvious place to look was the Castle, and that's what I told the police!'

Then you ask the ten million dollar question, 'But where is the Diamond?' Turn to **12**.

70

Lord Fairchild continues, 'I've arranged a little meeting with the burglars. They're holding your grandfather as a hostage and they want the Konchi Diamond in exchange for your grandfather's safe return. I had a replica made of the Konchi Diamond, so I'm going to give them that. That way we'll get your grandfather back and still have the real Konchi Diamond. Don't you think it's a wonderful idea?'

'Yes, yes, but isn't it a bit dangerous?' you ask.

Lord Fairchild says, 'Don't worry, I've contacted the police. They are hiding in the garden ready to arrest the burglars. What time is it? Half past two! They'll be here soon. Hide upstairs!'

You go into one of the bedrooms. Soon you hear the sound of a car arriving. Out of the window you can just see your grandfather with two men.

They come towards the house and ring the front doorbell.

At the same time as Lord Fairchild opens the door,

several policemen run out from behind the trees in the garden. There is a bit of a fight between the police and the burglars but soon everything is under control. The burglars are handcuffed and taken to the police car. The Chief Inspector comes into the house and says, 'Thank you Lord Fairchild for going through with this. At last we have arrested these two. We've been trying to catch them for years.'

When the Chief Inspector sees you he says, 'My goodness, you must be the grandson. The family resemblance is unmistakable. Well, this is a nice surprise, not only is the real Konchi Diamond safe and the burglars arrested, but this is also a family reunion. I'll leave you now so that you can catch up on all the news. Goodbye.'

You ask your grandfather to tell you all about the burglars. Lord Fairchild says, 'Yes, let's have a good cup of tea and we'll tell you all about it. Do you know, I always thought I'd make a good Sherlock Holmes.' You all burst out laughing.

71

You start going down the corridor. You hear the door close behind you. Somebody must be following you. You hide behind a door. You hear footsteps coming down the corridor. The door opens and there is your grandfather standing in front of you. You stare at

each other for a moment then hug each other. 'It's you,' you both say at the same time.

You explain what you have been doing since you came to England and then your grandfather begins his story. He says, 'I hid the Konchi Diamond here some years ago when I stayed here with Lord Fairchild. Some criminals have been trying to get the Konchi Diamond from me in exchange for the treasures they stole from Lord Fairchild. I hit on the brilliant idea of having a replica of the Konchi Diamond made. So when I met the criminals, I gave them the replica. It was all a trap and in fact the police caught them yesterday. That's why today I've come back for the real Konchi Diamond. Follow me.'

Above the fireplace in the hall, there are tiles in the shape of a diamond. Your grandfather carefully removes one of the tiles. There behind the tile is the Konchi Diamond. This is the happy end of your adventure. You have found your grandfather and the Konchi Diamond is safe.

'I think we should go home together now, don't you?' says your grandfather.

72

You walk around the rather charming little village. You look at all the different houses with interest, they seem completely different and rather foreign to you.

You try to feel some kind of connection with your surroundings. It is very difficult, and you just cannot stop thinking about the gypsy and her rather sinister message. The stone weighs heavily in your hand and it feels like ice. Suddenly, an old lady approaches you, 'Hello! I'm sorry to bother you but you must be Arthur's son or at least his grandson! You look so much like him. What are you doing here? Have you been to see Arthur?'

You look at her in surprise. What on earth is she talking about? Who is Arthur? You decide it is a good idea to find out some more information. She looks like a local lady, perhaps she can tell you more about the gypsy and the mysterious Arthur. Turn to **39**.

73

During the night you keep dreaming about your grandfather and the Konchi Diamond. In your dream, you keep seeing your grandfather in what looks like a cellar. The door is locked and he is a prisoner. Then you keep seeing the Konchi Diamond again and this image keeps dividing into two. You cannot really understand what this means. The dream leaves you restless and worried.

When you wake up the next morning, you decide to go for a walk in the village after breakfast. You feel as though you need some fresh air and some time to think things over.

As you are walking down the High Street, you see an interesting-looking shop. The sign above the door says 'Lapidary' and in the window there are lots of semi-precious stones: opals, quartz, topaz and so on. Then you remember the meaning of 'lapidary' – a person who cuts precious stones. There is a young girl working at a machine in the shop. You do not know why but you feel you should go into the shop. Turn to **11**.

74

You decided to ask the gardener a few questions. You ask him, 'Who is that?'

'Don't you know?' he replies, 'I would have thought that you, of all people, would know. You look just like him. He isn't, in fact, what he seems!'

You wonder what on earth this old gardener is talking about. He seems to be talking in riddles. You ask him again, 'Who is that? Is his name Arturo Romelli?'

He replies, 'His name is indeed Romelli but his first name is Jorge. He was Arturo's brother, his twin, in fact. Jorge is the person Arturo – or Arthur as he is known here – came to visit. Now that Jorge has been murdered, Arthur owns this house.'

This is all too much for you; first, you discover that you have a great-uncle that you never knew existed, then you discover that he has been murdered. You ask him, 'But why was he murdered? And where is Arthur?'

He answers, 'Come with me, I will take you to someone who can answer you better than I can.'

You feel very confused, you still do not know whether to trust him or not. If you decide to go with him, turn to **56**. If you decide not to go with him, turn to **42**.

75

Meanwhile, you have reached the point above which the Konchi Diamond is hovering. It is still giving out a very strong white light. Everyone turns to look at you and it. The Diamond falls very slowly, straight into your cupped hands. You gasp because it feels very cold, as cold as ice. Your grandfather comes over to you and hugs you. You have achieved your goal, you have found both your grandfather and the Konchi Diamond, the police have arrested the robbers and you feel very happy!

There is silence in the room. Finally, the gypsy says, 'That's how it should be! The Konchi Diamond is now back with its own family and that's where it should stay.' She looks at the policemen and the robbers and says, 'Remember, all those who try to steal the stone will die! Diamonds spell Danger!' This is the end of the adventure for you. You have succeeded. Well done!

76

Suddenly, the 'policeman' grabs your arm and says, 'OK kid, we know you must be Arthur's grandson and we've seen you going round Harminster asking all those questions. We are going to hide you to keep you out of the way for a while.'

He drags you to the Castle and takes you inside through a side door. He pushes you down into the cellars. It is very dark down there but as he pushes you into one of the rooms, you see another figure there. As your eyes are getting used to the darkness, the figure in the corner says, 'Is it really you?' You peer into the darkness and yes, there he is, your grandfather.

The 'policeman' says, 'We'll be back in a couple of hours when we've checked out your diamond, Arthur.' He then goes. You turn to your grandfather and ask, 'What's going on?'

Your grandfather explains that these robbers have been trying to get hold of the Konchi Diamond for a long time and that he had a replica made which he has given to the robbers. When the robbers find out it is only a replica there will be real trouble. The situation is desperate. Turn to **79**.

77

You feel really excited. At last you are getting some clues. You decide to ask Miss Lyon some very direct questions. She suggests going back to her cottage for a cup of cocoa. You agree gladly, this will give you all the opportunities to ask her all the questions you want answered.

Later, sitting in a comfortable armchair in front of a log fire, sipping your very English bedtime drink of cocoa, you say to Miss Lyon, 'What did Arthur look like?'

She replies, 'Oh, he was such a handsome man. He was very tall, dark and always most elegantly dressed. In fact, he always had a silk handkerchief in his top pocket and a red carnation in his button-hole! I really have no idea where he got them from, especially in the winter. And he was so interested in history. My goodness, he was a font of information, especially on . . . What's that, who's there?'

There is a very strange noise outside, almost as

though someone with a stick is walking heavily up to the front door. If you get up to go and see who is there, turn to **57**. If you say, 'Oh, it's nothing. It's just the wind!' turn to **49**.

78

You decide to try and find out something about the gypsy. The coincidences are just too much for you to accept so you decide to walk round the busy market square and ask the other stallholders about the gypsy.

You timidly approach a stall selling fruit and vegetables and stand in the queue. You buy a pound of apples and some grapes and then you say to the stallholder who looks like a typical English farmer, sturdy and red-cheeked, wearing fingerless gloves and a funny little hat, 'Excuse me, you know the gypsy selling uncut stones ...'

'I don't know any gypsy round here, do you Fred?' He turns to the man next to him; he shakes his head. You feel a bit silly and thank him and move on to the next stall. This stall is selling sweets but you feel you cannot ask the stallholder for information without first buying something. So you buy some sweets that you do not particularly want and ask the same questions. No one has any information. The same thing happens at the next two stalls you visit. You have a lot of unwanted purchases but you draw a complete blank. Either they do not know the answers to your questions or they do not want to tell you. You decide to walk back to where the gypsy's stall was. Turn to **63**.

79

'I really don't know what we are going to do when the robbers find out that the diamond they have is only a replica,' your grandfather says.

'Can't we try to escape?' you ask.

'It's no use. I've already tried,' your grandfather says. Just then you hear a knocking and thumping, terrible crashes and bangs. You wonder what on earth is going on. Then you hear someone shouting, 'Hello, is anyone there? This is the police.'

You cannot believe your luck. You both begin to shout, 'Here we are in the cellar.'

There is another terrible crash as somebody breaks down the door to the cellars. Within seconds, two policemen are standing in the doorway smiling at you. Of course your grandfather's first question is, 'How did you find us?'

'We just followed your grandson. We heard that he'd been asking questions about you in the village so we thought we'd better keep an eye on him. He led us to you. You'll also be glad to hear that we have arrested the robber who just left here. Doubtless he'll lead us to the other robbers. They're part of a big international diamond smuggling ring. By the way, I hope the real Konchi Diamond is safe, is it?' the policeman asks.

'Don't worry, I've hidden it here in the house,' your grandfather says.

And you, the hero of our adventure, you have found your grandfather and saved the Konchi Diamond from these terrible robbers. Well done!

80

You stand there motionless, rooted to the spot. The gypsy says, 'Come quickly, into the secret passage. We must go back to the Manor House and get the Konchi Diamond. Someone must have followed me here or perhaps they were watching the Castle. Quickly, we don't have a moment to lose!' She runs over to the small door and opens it. You are absolutely frozen with fear, you do not know what to do. If you decide to follow the gypsy, turn to **30**. If you are too frightened to move, turn to **23**.

81

Suddenly, you hear someone whispering, 'Psst, over here. Psst, psst.'

Oh, no! The last time you heard someone call you like that, you got hit on the head. You could move, by rolling from side to side, to the part of the cellar where the noise is coming from. What are you going to do? You are after all in quite a desperate situation. How are you going to find your grandfather now? Are you even going to get out of this alive? If you decide to move towards the place where someone is trying to attract your attention, turn to **28**. If you decide you would be safer staying where you are, turn to **83**.

82

You arrange to see Chief Inspector Barnes at 2 p.m. the following afternoon. When you arrive you are shown into a large, well-lit office on the top floor. There is an enormous picture window which gives a wonderful view of London. But you are not here to admire the view!

The Chief Inspector begins, 'I thought I'd better see you straight away as we are at a very delicate point in our investigation into your grandfather's dis-appearance. Some extremely nasty criminals, the

Bray Brothers, have been trying to get hold of the Konchi Diamond. We are sure they are holding your grandfather hostage somewhere. Lord Fairchild has had a replica of the Konchi Diamond made so that we can set a trap for the Bray Brothers.

'I'm telling you all this in the strictest confidence so that you realize you must not interfere in our work. I want you to stay in London and stop trying to find your grandfather. In a few days we will find him and as soon as that has happened, we will phone you and you can be reunited. Do you understand the importance of what I'm saying?'

'Yes,' you reply. If you stay in a hotel in London and wait for the police to phone you, turn to **68**. If you go back to Harminster and go to the Castle yourself, turn to **45**.

83

You decided to stay where you are. You think you have taken too many risks already, so you are going to play safe. However, the person who has been calling you continues to whisper, 'Psst, psst!'

Suddenly you hear footsteps. It sounds as though a lot of people are coming towards the cellar. All at once, the door bursts open and several policemen charge into the room. You find it difficult to move but the person who has been trying to attract your attention can move. You discover that it was Miss Lyon! She runs over to the policemen and explains the situation. After a lot of talking, and after they have untied you, you and Miss Lyon are driven away in a police car.

As you drive into the village, you notice that everybody is watching you; people are standing around in the street, and others are looking at you from behind lace curtains and so on. Your search for your grandfather and the Konchi Diamond is obviously no longer a secret, you decide you might as well give up. You are tired and fed up and you decide that someone else can carry on the search. You take the next plane home. This is the end of your adventure. ■

84

You follow the gardener into the house. It is a beautiful old house, with high ceilings, interesting, uneven walls and with a lot of wood everywhere. You would like to have a better look round but the gardener walks through the rooms without giving you a chance to look closely at anything. He finally stops outside the door of what must be the main room. He turns round and looks at you and says, 'I think you'll recognize this picture!' and walks into a very large room. At the far end of the room, above the

fireplace, there is a portrait hanging on the wall. It is your grandfather, painted standing outside this house.

You are shocked, you look closely at the painting; it is definitely him. You ask yourself what on earth your grandfather was doing here. In the portrait, he looks as though he were the owner of this place. How can this be?

The gardener is standing beside you, obviously waiting for you to say something. You really want to ask him lots of questions. It you decide to go ahead and ask him everything you want to know, turn to **74**. If you decide that you cannot ask him anything because you do not know him and you do not understand what is happening, turn to **10**.

85

As soon as you take his gag off, your grandfather begins to speak, 'Thank goodness you've found me. I can't believe it's you. What are you doing here and how did you find me?'

You tell him all about your dream when you were at home and all your adventures in England. 'But grandfather, why are you here like this?' you ask.

Your grandfather begins to explain everything. He says, 'The owner of this Castle, Lord Fairchild, is in fact a distant relative of ours and I came here to stay with him a few years ago. At that time some burglars got into the Castle and stole lots of family treasures. All these things are of great value and importance to the family. Lord Fairchild was so heartbroken that he moved out of the Castle and went to live in a nearby village.

'Some time later a note came from the burglars. They had obviously found out about me and the Konchi Diamond because the note said: *"Unless you give us the Konchi Diamond, we will melt down all the gold and silver so that we can sell it."*

'This of course presented us with a real dilemma. The family treasures are irreplaceable but so is the Konchi Diamond. Finally Lord Fairchild and I decided on a plan. We had a replica of the Konchi Diamond made to give to the burglars. We thought that we would be able to get the family treasures back and keep the real Konchi Diamond. I agreed to meet the burglars here to give them the "diamond". When I met them they tied me up and put me here in the cellar. They said they wanted to check to see if the diamond was real or not before giving me the

gold and silver. You have come in the nick of time. You've probably saved my life. Let's go to the police for help. By the way, I've hidden the real Konchi Diamond in the walled garden.'

So this is the happy ending to your adventure. Here is your grandfather; the Konchi Diamond is safe and the police are sure to catch the burglars.

86

You decided to go and have tea with your new acquaintance from the market, Miss Lyon.

She seems to be a rather charming old lady who looks somewhat like the Queen Mother which makes you trust her immediately. When you arrive at her house, you discover that it is a typical English cottage. It is an old building, with a thatched roof, that has been extended to double its original size; it looks large and rambling.

Your hostess greets you as you arrive, 'Do come in, my dear. Let me take your jacket, I'd like you to feel at home. Come and sit down in Arthur's favourite chair. You look as though you belong there.'

You feel quite intrigued. What is she going to tell you about Arthur? The old lady brings in a tray of tea things, then goes and gets a plateful of cucumber sandwiches.

You sit and chat, drinking tea and eating sand-

wiches. She does not say much that is of interest to you; however, a lot of what she says contains references to Arthur. When you ask her direct questions, she never seems to be able to answer you. You find this very irritating and you feel quite pleased when she says, 'Would you like to come and have a walk with me? Arthur and I often used to go for walks in the evenings and we always went to the same place, Devil's Point!'

You feel rather excited, you no longer feel bored. You stand up and say, 'Yes, I'd love to!' You walk down towards Devil's Point. Turn to **54**.

87

Miss Lyon has just sneezed. The two men, who are obviously criminals, jump in surprise.

'Over there, Jim, quick! I'll go this way,' says one of them.

They separate and are now running in the direction of the sneeze and Miss Lyon. You cannot let them get the old lady without doing something about it. You jump up and shout, 'Over here!'

You pull the stone out of your pocket; it is vibrating and feels very hot in your hand. The strange light is coming from it again, you focus the light beam on the two robbers and hope to goodness that it works in the same way as it did on the mouse.

It does! The criminals stop dead in their tracks; They cannot move; it seems as if they are hypnotized.

'Oh, well done!' shouts Miss Lyon, as she walks towards you. 'Just keep the light beam on them! The police should be here in a minute!'

'But when did you call the police? How did you know where I was? How do you know about the stone? What is this stone?' The questions just keep tumbling out. Miss Lyon laughs and says, 'Later, later. I'll tell you later.' Turn to **50**.

GLOSSARY

agile able to move quickly and easily

animatedly in a lively way

coat of arms special symbol of an aristocratic family, university etc.

to have the courage of your convictions to believe what you are doing is right

desolate lonely and deserted

to do away with to get rid of

dot; back to the year dot a long time ago

to draw a complete blank to get no information

dumpy a bit overweight

flash; in a flash quickly

foolhardy taking unnecessary risks

foolish silly

foothold a place to put your foot, especially when climbing

funny goings on strange happenings

to gag to cover someone's mouth so that they cannot speak

the game is up you have been discovered

to gasp to breathe in loudly in shock or surprise

to get cold feet to become afraid

to go with to match (of clothes), to look good together

to graze to cause a surface wound, to break the skin slightly for instance when you fall

gutturally speak in a low voice from the throat

handcuffs metal rings put on the wrists of criminals

to hand over to give

to hit on an idea to have an idea

to hop in to get in

to hover to stay up in the air without moving

immobilized unable to move

infamous well known for something bad

intrigued very interested

irritating annoying

ivy a type of plant which climbs up walls

jumpy nervous

lapis lazuli a type of blue stone

to melt down to make liquid by heating, especially of metals

moss a small flat green plant which grows in a thick mass

in the nick of time just in time

nimble on her feet able to move quickly and easily

non-starter something which will never work

omen a sign that something is going to happen in the future

opal a type of precious stone

paralysed unable to move

to peer to look closely at something

poacher someone who shoots or catches animals etc without permission

to prick up your ears to listen very carefully

to prune to cut the branches of a tree or bush

to ramble to chat about nothing in particular

reluctantly the way you do something you do not want to do

to rip to tear

rustling a sound made when something light moves

sinister evil

to slam the door to close the door violently

to sort out to solve

stroll a walk

swim; your head is swimming your head is going round and round

thatched roof a roof made of straw

timid shy

troubled worried

to turn up to arrive

turret a small tower

undergrowth bushes, plants etc.

to vanish to disappear